Saint Worm

SAINT WORM

POEMS BY

Hailey Leithauser

ABLE MUSE PRESS

Able Muse Press

www.ablemusepress.com

Printed in the United States of America

Library of Congress Control Number: 2019937307

ISBN 978-1-77349-045-8 (paperback)
ISBN 978-1-77349-084-7 (hardcover)
ISBN 978-1-77349-046-5 (digital)

Cover image: "Woman with Bowler Hat" by Gonzalo Fuenmayor (38 x 50 in, charcoal on paper, 2014, courtesy of Gonzalo Fuenmayor and Dolby Chadwick Gallery, SF)

Cover & book design by Alexander Pepple

Able Muse Press is an imprint of *Able Muse*: A Review of Poetry, Prose & Art—at www.ablemuse.com

Able Muse Press
467 Saratoga Avenue #602
San Jose, CA 95129

This book is dedicated to the memory of

Charles Henry Leithauser

Acknowledgments

My grateful acknowledgments go to the editors of the following publications where these poems, some in earlier versions, first appeared:

32 Poems: "The Pickpocket Song"

Able Muse: "*Rrribbit*," "The Hangman's Song," "Sin-Eater Worm," and "Postmortem Consortium" (under the title "Sex after Death")

Agni: "I Shall Name the Worms," "Fat Worm," and "To the North Wind"

Agni Online: "Coronation" and "The Distance of Objects"

Antioch Review: "Crows" and "Eminent Worm"

Crazyhorse: "Eurydice"

Ecotone: "Monster," "Saint Worm," "Dumb Luck," "Poke," and "Coy Worm"

Field: "Midnight," "Slow Danger"

The Gettysburg Review: "Message," "Mad Tom," and "Mad Maudlin"

Image: "Some Small Bone" and "Glowworm"

Innisfree: "Murder Song" and "[Bring me the head]"

The Journal: "*Hsss*"

Margie: "Octopus"

Pleiades: "Mary," "Angels," and "The Cannibal's Song"

Poet Lore: "Moley's Chair"

Poetry: "Arrhythmia," "Albino," and "0"

River Styx: "Minnows"

The Southwest Review: "In My Last Past Life"

Sou'wester: "White on White"

The Yale Review: "Bookworm," "Tollund," and "Wanderlusts"

"Some Small Bone" and "White on White" were featured on *Poetry Daily*.

"In My Last Past Life" appeared in *The Best American Poetry 2014*, Terence Hayes, editor.

"The Pickpocket Song" appeared in *The Best American Poetry 2015*, Sherman Alexie, editor.

Massive gratitude to the many people, including AB, SB, DK, GM, SR, and KY, whose critical eyes and general bucking up were of incalculable help in getting this book done, to Gonzalo Fuenmayor for the generous use of his stunning artwork, and to Alex Pepple and the good people of Able Muse Press.

"Slow Danger" is dedicated to Deborah Bogan.

"The Pickpocket Song" was an experiment in shared lines with, and is dedicated to, Amy Beeder.

"Moley's Chair" is dedicated to Diana B. Kuhl who gave me, finally, in my dotage, a copy of *The Wind in the Willows*.

Contents

Then you were happy, when you could still tremble

— Louis Simpson

Saint Worm

Arrhythmia

The heart of a bear is a cloud-shuttered
mountain. The heart of a mountain's a kiln.
The white heart of a moth has nineteen white
chambers. The heart of a swan is a swan.

The heart of a wasp is a prick of plush.
The heart of a sloth gathers moss. The heart
of an owl is part blood and part chalice.
The fey mouse heart rides a dawdy dust-cart.

The heart of a kestrel hides a house wren
at nest. The heart of a lark is a czar.
The heart of a scorpion holds swidden

and spark. The heart of a shark is a gear.
Listen and tell, thrums the grave heart of humans.
Listen well love, for it's pitch dark down here.

* * *

Some Small Bone

Some small bone in your foot is longing for heaven
—Robert Bly

This twinge at first stir
too modest for throb,
more diffident
than tug,
not an itch,
not the most
incurious twitch
of a hook,
not a jerk,
but the tease
of brustle
of the fine, stiff pinions
of every curtained
saint and cherub.

Octopus

Most entangled
and limb burdened, buoyed smoke- and ghost-
and Christ-like in reluctant temperament,
citizens of crevices
and small lost pots,

they lack panache.
Once my mother made one of a wash-
cloth laced with blood and clay. Twelve years later
on a cold Tribeca bar-
room barstool in

a lean, gin-bright
Easter Sunday morning lull, I ate
two diced and salted on a shell thin plate
of pale, petal-stenciled trim
and orchid white.

I Shall Name the Worms

worms are the words but joy's the voice
—e.e. cummings

I shall name the worms
        who feast on me:
    Eloise and Dot,
Old Alphonse,
            and Cecily.
What shivaree
this mob shall see!
        —my lithesome Dot
            and spotted Eloise,
    and kicking off
        his crutches, what
palatial bacchanal
    for Old Alphonse
with never far behind
    divine,
        intemperate,
    dear Cecily.
They will have
        a tambourine
    or three,
        a painted set
    of antique
castanets
        and emblemed
    bugles bright

as winter sun.
   Their dance
will start, for once,
  at one
  and last until
it's time for tea when
   they may pause their
  clubby folderol to
ask,
I wonder what poor sap
  has set us
to this task—
a secretary, cook,
  a cop, a cellist,
 a micrologist?
 And
  did she
 ever dance as we
or sing or fling
  her questions at the stars
with eyes as wide
  as plum jam jars?
 Did she often stop
  at evening light
 to watch a bat
  or laugh beneath
the gentling
  of a trembled willow
 tree? Did she

place love in
her palm, or did
she roam in rain
alone?
The moon will rise,
  the sea will sigh,
      the freckled smile
of Eloise will widen
    as she chomps,
  and Old Alphonse and Dot
    will flap their gums
        in a confederate
fair harmony
  echoed by a single,
    softened
        afterthought, wafting
late, one half-
flat note,
unshepherded, almost
    unheard
  and unperceived,
          from tiddled,
  gassy Cecily.

Hsss

Whether pricked inner tube,
snake uncharming or flat
eared cat, it's still warning.
Now's not the time
to contemplate
fate or delve in
mused amusings
on the clocking
of twitching or
gauging of reach.
Better to circle
wagons, fireproof
bridges, bulwark all
frail fortresses, hone
pitchforks and torches
before sibilance
answers the cue to
rain war upon you.

Ouroboros

Ouroboros, old chap,
made of his ass a snack,

and of that made a wheel
in which he bended all

unnumbered, vaporous seas
to summed infinities

beginning with his end,
again, again, again.

Midnight

The problem with midnight is
that it never rains then,
not even in spring when the old
roots dig in
or in summer when the tangled up
woods get angry
and the windows are all left stupidly open.
At dinner, it softens the pane
in a silk gray of mirrors
or sometimes right before dawn
low-lying clouds reconvene in a coven;
lightning quivers and thunder
shakes and echoes the timber.
But night after night
as the moon weeps the meridian
and the soundless pendulum swings
mid-point,
at the light's most mortal hour,
it's a drought,
sere, sere, as a cotton-seed sprout.
And you know,
and you know,
as you know your own soul,
that that is not right.

Rrribbit

So rarely does music
so clearly resemble
the creature who makes it.
Wrens and sparrows
sorrow larger,
the giant sloth,
goliath bird-
eating spider
cry out smaller,
than they all are.
It's only the toad
consigned to her squat,
mud green, pot-shaped house,
fattening on flies,
who tries a nocturne
of such dense remorse
that it exhibits
commensurate size.

Bookworm

(*Larva of the* Xestobium rufovillosum, *or Deathwatch Beetle*)

This is the
stuff, the bright
purple juice
a pawn of
the grape
could blither
and faint
for swilling
and swallowing
vowel and
consonant,
macron,
háček, ogonek
and umlaut,
confounding
the mouth
with curlicue, dot,
strait Roman
numeral, serif
and loop;
this is the
gist, salty
and salty
and sweet,
the chewing,
the sate—
Garamond,

Blackadder,
Pristina, Script;
here is
the clambake,
potlatch,
a shinny, a picnic,
a barbecue, blow-
out, stick
a fork
in it slowly,
so slowly let
each perfect
word steep
brown in its paper,
let paper be
pulp, let pulp
be pastiche,
let grist
greet the gullet,
bowel
bless it
solemnly;
there is
room for us,
place,
there is space for
the ages,
we're all scribbled
on water,
bring, bring
out
the dead.

White on White

    Rug dropped sugar,
fresh, wet iris on marble dresser,
the chopping of combers under cold sun,
   rain-faded boards of proud, paint-
     poor churches, great

    dumb snows hiding
inside clouds hidden inside sky. Bring
two together and we see the old lot
   of language to ledger tint
     from tone, hint from

    whisper (not quite
sauterne, closer to crisper champagne),
to cite complement, how as a snail stains
   a cement path, the pearled trace
     kindles in light.

Murder Song

Clack, chatter,
Rattle, rasp, rattle:

Off at midnight
West to shallows

Squall, caw, caw, cackle:
Over meadow, tor, moorland

Natter, scratch, croak, scratch, prattle:
Graveyard, garth, haycock, cradle.

In My Last Past Life

In my last past life I had a nut brown wife,
a gray and white house looking over the sea,
a forest for love and a river for grief,

a goshawk for beauty, for courage a knife,
a city for distance, lights spread on the sea.
In my last past life I had a brown wife

subtle and busy and contented and brief
(she stood in the dusk silhouette with the sea),
a forest and love and a river, and grief

was a ghost hidden green in the leaves,
an echo off cliffs that bound back the sea.
In my life it would last, my past and my wife,

the wrens in the garden, the moon on the roof,
day winds that flirted and teased at the sea,
the forest that loved and the river that grieved

the life that was garden and day wind and thief
(each sunrise and sundown the turn of the sea),
the life that I had, and my last brown wife,
a forest for love, a still river for grief.

Slow Danger

(Road Sign)

Snakes for example when the heat
  off the patio slate makes them lazy,
or some sluggish, deliberate fungus
  or butter-fed heart operating just slightly
    off-beat.
              It's a cheat
when it jumps out so fast you can't
  grimace, can't think, only shriek:
    Death! Death!
                   there in the right
  lane, there on the scaffolding,
after the ice-crack, half down the stairs,
    so unfair
to ambush with a club—how much
  nicer, politer, are the well-mannered
amyloid spatters, those quietly shy
  gray triglycerides, how very less
  worried, less harried, your fate
and the stretch of its long, deep,
              calculable
  evenings of reason preceding
with no hurry to spell out or dwell on
  their red-flagged conclusion.

Glowworm

I am the whisper
matches rattle
in their cold
and cardboard hovels.
I'm desire
gone to ground.
I am efficient,
almost secret;
you can read in me
such scripture
of the most compacted
and contented
red light district.
Impish sample seraph,
humblest in lust
I am the apocryphalest
rumor waiting
just around the corner.
Seek and see me
meekly, simmer;
I am bright and quiet;
I am blithe and ardent;
I am softly, briefly
urging: Garner in
my hand-cupped spark
and I will make
your faring warmer,
yearnful, closer,
wider, darker.

Monster

Many nights I talk in silence to the stars.
Only I and the dim, distant fires,

none else to throw a shadow on the shadowed ground.

Some hearts rest a smaller roof, a closer fire,
the warmth of other voices sung to nearer ears.
Evening, soft black wool pulled neat beneath the chin,

rain, a bog-bred thief, tethering dark to wind.

The Pickpocket Song

Tickle a backside, pal, fiddle the wrist,
hither then sterling, then amethyst, onyx.
Eager spills eel-skin, python, seal-leather,
platinum and plate, all cabbage, all cheddar.
I say to the cutpurses: Straighten, and sing. Let us
carol each quick sticky digit, all ten, for my
kith can fleece your kin, and then some,
proudly and soundly, down sheer to the skin.

Only we dippers can psalm such a trilling,
cash-clips and coppers, all harmony belling.
Keen-fingered lifters, join in with them—
each bracelet, each necklace, each pearl-circled pin,
topaz and lapis, square perfect carats
swearing their ritzier whisper and pinch,
over and over the nimble thumb-catch.
Noble this music, good, noble, and able.
Grandeur for soul, chums, glad glory for table.

The Hangman's Song

They say that Heaven is sodden with light;
just Heaven and Earth and six feet to go,
just Earth and Heaven and ten little toes
ruffled and fluttered in ten tidy rows.

They say that the way is doddering flight,
a lurch and a jigger, and left between
the clouds and cold ground stays a creaking thing
of wood and of air and of greasy string,

not collecting the sky, but getting close,
with graupel and snow blowing up his nose.

Saint Worm

A fête for
fleas,
perhaps,
or nits,
but for the rest
of us he
was a piteous dis-
appointment
(some
skin, more
bone,
his gut a
bust, his
cranium
a silent
drum, his
Heart
already
torched to
cinders
spent
as winter,
testicles
two bitter
marbles,
the
pith of him

all that we
found,
less a stone,
not half
a pound),
although
I must
at least
admit,
despite the sauce,
his milky
alabaster
box was
posh.

Albino

A lot more of than thought, unsought, come out white.
Lemurs of Madagascar, and leopards sans spots.

Brilliant, I think, to spurn pigment and burn
in December light, a December filament.

No one would know if there's snow in your hair,
or whether or not, when they knock, you are there.

Coronation

All hail the noggin with the diadem!
All hail they who may some day
be snipped or snapped
off at the stem.
For though they be fodder in
training, wouldn't you, even
with slaughter a credible wrinkle
if given the shot,
the one time door knock,
to glide down the gangways of
censers and wobbly miters,
the tremble-
hand candles, oh,
wouldn't you, just,
so lost among organs and trumpets
and silver-thread,
embroidered orchids
with no born-to-it,
heretofore glimmer or sense
of noblesse,
wouldn't you, trusting,
alone, slip on
the welterweight topper
and sing swank as an opera
from the buttery
lamplights of Moscow to Rome?

Tollund

This is death, bleary as the dying was,
half slop on the bottom, half stew
on the top, half forgotten wren
evening song, tiny and timeless bird singing.
This is death when you don't have a breath
or a pulse or a voice but still
have two lungs and a rubbery heart to breathe
in and out of,
less of a death than a settling,
less of a settling than press
under the march of feet feet feet foot
that nobody knows a dying
dead man is deeply and darkly and quietly
privy to (marking
a calendar
of sour nosed worms, acidic
maggots, slug, beetle, grub
at nest in a tibia they will never grow
fat on). This is a death
that crows want to honor and snow
at rest on gentling hills wants to lie over.
This death that is weariness,
this death that is meaningless
and careful experience,
that is glacial and graveled, hoveled experience
like that of existence (calling of children
over millennia, loud rivers,
clouds). This is the palaces

of children and clouds, days made
of fingers and brown brittle ferns,
nights made of phosphorus,
stale water stench. This is the blanch
of a close, stagnant pyre,
the burning of soft-bodied amber,
the cargo of stomach, the plenty of gut.
This is the roughed and the untidy peace
of a mud-sodden stuff.
This is the death the living are made of.

Eurydice

A common button, a tooth, a tattoo
of a flamingo, a cold swallowed tear.

Ordinarily I've nothing to wear.

A mannered stranger: was it simply you?

You're back in the dark of your room, dreaming
of a well-pressed suit, an electric fan,
dogs arguing, a vague fornication.

Was this then your heart, its ruinous hinge?

Rain gestures slowly, gibbering of siege.

It had an allure I am aware of—
love's pimple, love's stumble, love's leaky roof,

and after, throttled laughter caught offstage,
in the distance a trawling, then blind strike,

then jerk and gaff and gored breach into light.

Mary

Like an off-kilter blister
the sea preening for storm.

It's warm. Clouds fluster
and blemish,

wasps scuttle, act skittish.
I'm cold.

I'm singing a tune
in my head

that's muddling the light
that's speckling the flock

of goats gone to rut.
They're slit-eyed in heat,

shit-streaked and unholy.
I'm not

in my right mind today.
Aunt says a red

dusk sours the wine, invites
tousled succubae down

from the attic.
She's old.

Last night a moon came,
dove-fat and augured,

into my room. I kissed it,
curling my pillow

and kicking the sheet.
Now at my feet

lies such puddle
of feathers. Forgive me.

Angels

are not your feathery
friends. When they cry sometimes,
eminent bridges go down,
and when they waddle
the earth, small
towns become great
indentations.
They husband a wrong
fondness for salt
hauled out in incalculable
sacks on mountainous
shoulders. Trashed,
they pee into oceans.
Their voices, though
gorgeous, often din coarse
and disengage ashes;
when they speak
men break,
women turn dead
or tally up gravid.

Sin-Eater Worm

A sturdy, well-set fellow,
   the mellow sort
who'd pluck a kitten
      from a tree
         or walk
   a zig-zagged, rain-
         soaked bully-
      ragging bibber
ten blocks to his door.
         Adding to
   his credit, unlike
      most he had an unfeigned
smile still fixed within
   the fleshy dark
pink swelling of his
         lip, an absence
   of vexation in the rimples
of his brow. There
      was a scent, un-
dimmed, about the
            weathered
vest and handkerchief
   of candle wax and
leafy juniper and strange
   to say, despite the rising
wind and snows the
      roses laid on

top his box were piled
        so deeply, the
tissues dropped so thick,
        I thought at first
I'd stumbled on
the catafalque of some sea-
        mauled, sea-
    battered hero brought
        at last to rest or
            barring that then new
                remains of
an unspotted child.

The Cannibal's Song

Today I found some flowers, three, in a row.

Yellow, yellow, yellow.

How poetic it made me feel, all of that sunlight pouring
evenly into their beggars' mouths, into the brave, beggarly
cups of their hands.

Another man or woman might have walked on past,
not stopping to notice the mouths,
not stopping to notice the hands,
interested only in her own internal life,
biting his lip against the yellow brightness,

however,

as I may have mentioned, I have the soul of a poet.
Love of the world fills me as rain fills a battered rain barrel.

So much love that I carry a small knife wherever I go,
so much love I carry a small, silver fork, a spoon,
ornate and profound cutlery spilling from my pockets,
napkins, salt and pepper shakers, a Murano glass,
graceful to the hand, etched with shepherds and cloud-colored lamb.

0

Philosophic
in its complex, ovoid emptiness,
a skillful pundit coined it as a sort
of stopgap doorstop for those
quaint equations

Romans never
dreamt of. In form completely clever
and discrete—a mirror come unsilvered,
loose watch face without the works,
a hollowed globe

from tip to toe
unbroken, it evades the grappling
hooks of mass, tilts the thin rim of no thing,
remains embryonic *sum*,
non-*cogito*.

Message

Beware it friend.
Beware it now,

beware it then.
Beware

its steps upon
the stair. Beware

what jiggles
handles at

your door, what
twists the rugs

of hallway floors.
Beware

boudoirs,
their soft-ticked dark;

be scared of all that
treads outdoors. Take

guard, take time,
take caution as

you cautious
climb. Approach

with dread what you once
dared; take sense

in all that stirs
in air. Take in each

tiny step, great
care.

Let autumn come,
let summer

go, let spring shake
off its weight

of snow. Be
bare once more,

know fear,
old friend.

Be wary
as you go again.

The Distance of Objects

Found poem, from Lawrence Edwards, The Spangled Heavens, *1951*

Someone on another hill.
It is best not to look
straight at them. Observe them

out of the corner of your eye

like looking at a view from a railway carriage
in the absolute stillness and silence.

They seem to be almost touching one another,
the Old Moon in the New Moon's Arms,

the distance of objects very far away.

Perhaps you have sometimes looked up
at the sky, a piece of black glass.

All this time the light is sinking.

The natural question to ask is:
if you were out on a dark night,
if you walked toward them.

The natural question to ask:
if we are quite alone,
if we lived through the cold.

Wanderlusts

Mercury

My vitreous planet, louche
element, my wee dearest god;

Ruby-throat fevers
clamber and plummet,
upswing and summit, dive like a stone.

Reason abandons, abandons, abandons.

Youngblood goes Maying, sobbed grave to the bone.

Venus

Vesper-lit, as myrtle-hat virgins
enchanted by sermons, limb by limb loosened,

not horny, but moral, till dawn-spun

underskin blossom, then O
so vice-lovely, four-ace dice tumble.

Luna

Love is a mirror
useless as prayer,

new as a storm sea,
admired blindly.

Mars

Men like their arts (as Venus her darts)
and red is a Rubicon lust-deep and crossed

reveling sun-tilt of helmets, their long pointy props—

Sanguineous lads! Right-foot quick march!

Jupiter

Jackhammer blather vexes the night—
    upheaval's the patter, the
      patter's the *pater*
  illluminatum, from tip-
    top to bottom,
 extremum
   rex.

Saturn

Seven days, and one gets a season,
albeit a bleak one, of sate.
At least

there's a torch in the tunnel,
(urgent, rebutting), at least we can

recreate yew-bright and roses
nibbled by now to a crumb on the plate.

Pluto

Poof—you're demoted. You are trash, you are
looted. *Whoosh*—you are suckered, you're plucked
up to your elbows, you're circling the farm.

Take a glance in the glass, kid, there's no one around;

only heat rises, we're headed downtown.

Dumb Luck

When a punch is ducked
by a fall-down drunk,

or the bank is broke
by a card shark's blink,

then you know it's struck
like the tinny plink

of a rusted clock.
Such a timely plink,

and we're back in swank
with our shamrocks plucked,

with our baskets dunked,
with the caromed crack

of a dead stroke whack
and all eight balls sunk.

Crows

Because they are clever, we believe they are wise.
Because they are wise, we conclude they are good,

or evil, or good and evil, but never muddied
in between. Because they are arrant, are utter black,

we assume them to be downright chummy with death,
and so in England once a woman was pressed between stones

for owning a pillow made from crow feathers.
This, the people said, gave her the power to dream affliction

like moonlight into the lives of their children,
and even though during her trial, records show

that the streets rang with the din of fat and ruddy
lineage, there was still a principle involved

and the city was cheered when no crows arrived at her grave,
which was hurriedly and spotlessly dissembled by snow.

Fat Worm

We fat all creatures else to fat us, and we fat ourselves for maggots
—William Shakespeare

What lived a
cabbage-
coddled pet
will flesh, I've
found, the
tenderest
of pancreas,
and capon stewed
a day in
Beaujolais now
greases sweet a
spleen. All praise
the soul who
raised
the duck (Long
Island, turned
to Peking
stuffed) that
lumped
the knee and
spread the
neck, and Psalms
Be Sung
from town to

town for
those who braised
the chick
and fished
the trout that
made ballows
of her dimpled
jowls and
gave her
teeming
toe the gout.

Moley's Chair

All for the love and the flutter of a custard,
for the slosh of a chowder, its dunk-stir and sopping,
all for the reverence of bread crust,
the palming and weight of an egg with a spatter of pepper,
box-ground and pungent, freckling and stinging,
for the warming of cider with spices
and bourbon, and butter,
and for the love, not less,
of the *Times* and the *Globe* and a dozen
dozen *Reviews*,
I call out for the dusk and its dimmet,
the casting of flame-light,
the climbing and etchings of flame-light;
all for two elbows, a lap rug
and grateful repose of untroubled
buttocks, I give praise for its cushions, cushion its coil;
for a mustard and cracker and dry Spanish port,
for the blended, deep breath
of fruitlessness, sluggardness,
I hold in my prayers its tassels and wrinkles,
anoint with soft drool its patches and stain,
guard in my heart its orange, threadbare
chrysanthemums,
the petals and sepals of each oversized,
nacreous-veined,
blanched and embroidered,
burst-gusset burgundy rose.

Minnows

Minimal fishes,
        unglamorous
I sing to your inch length, muddy-colored
    never glimmering; name you
        nothing bright or numinous,
    oceanic or ambitious;
        whisper (lung-fat sister I) be not pan-cook
sought, but persist, deficient tenant of the hook.

Poke

Better the glorious
roar than
a dank,
clammy breath
on the neck,
brighter the teeth
when surly
and snow-
white and neat,
and surpassing
by star and light year
the thistle
and burr, the needle
and prick,
over bicker
or buffering, blusterous
sneer,
is the lure
of the tumbledown cage
and the bear
and the stick.

[Bring me the head]

Bring me the head
of the angel whose candle
you read by. Bring me
the photograph
of your first last kiss.

Don't try to tell me
your flesh is empyreal,
my body a shell. Bring

me your hairbrush
the color of honey,
a dark caramel swan
for when we are dead.

Coy Worm

No apples
   on a winter
tree,
  no peach, no nectarine,
no
   plum (not
even prunes
  among
   the never
ruined), no,
     no thing (a
    dust-
  thick tongue,
   and be-
neath the bosom,
  little
   lush) I
  could call
     marvelous
   within this
  mealy-
     flagged,
      undented
  tundra

that I should
swap quite
happily
for one well-
padded, bon-
bon stuffed,
contented, love-
wet
wife or
whore at
rest in
her more
bounteous,
benefic
bed.

Postmortem Consortium

Mr. and Mrs.
　　McClatter,
the Right Honorable
　Rattle,
　　Mistress and Master
Apparatus
　　down deep
in their catacombs,
　in boarded up
closets, unvisited attics
　　they're at it
　through thick
　　pink insulation,
　through cobweb, in
　　pillowing
　　　dust. How
　narrow they tangle
who once burrowed
　　vast-bellied,
　scrumptious-
　　　tallowed,
now whereby they puss-
　　purr and
　　　cosset, cradle
and blandish
　with spindles of clavicle,
angular scapula,

radius, capitate,
swiveling mandible,
        all of their marveling
    relish come
back catawampus, contoured
        and lumpless,
    with candy-coat
        kisses stripped down
    to whistle, fluttering
            flute-notes,
    knee-
knocks, choral tattooing,
        an eternal,
satyric jangle, fatless,
        unlarded,
the compassing ardor
    no longer flesh-
        muffled
but ossein-locking, by
        gristle pink-
tickled, in perpetuum.

Bedlam Songs

Mad Tom

Many are gibbers and many are sopwit
and many's a penny compared to Mad Tom.
Down on the hillock, up in the bog,
tilt-eye and hop foot, fox tails and rag;
Open mouth Tom, head like a honeycomb,
music like loblolly stuck to the tongue.

Some kissers squall, but my maw can chorus,
says cup-rattle addle-lad, Abraham-Man;
On with the wind-whip that swindles the hollow;
Never the dandy-cant, always codswallop:
Gobsmack and psalm-knot sings Bedlam's Old Tom.

Mad Maudlin

Bishops will pox you, and chats swing you high.
Make me a mansion, I'll sweep out a sty.
Add on a roof and I'll thatch you a sky
up to the clouds where the dead chaveys lie.

Draw me a nipper, I'll drink the cask dry.
Ask me an answer, I'll tell you a why.
If you spot me a tan, I'll square you five
and smile such a smile the blue bottles cry.

When winter burns summer, when blind cobs fly
and char-girls drink cream and eat sweet mince pies,
when the nights glow bright and gullies grow wise

and gads are hallowed and bawds sanctified,
on that day of days, at the turn of tides—
Grant me one wish and I'll be fair Bedlam's bride.

Eminent Worm

Gray, yes,
and greasy in
  spots (as was
    rumored by
  those in the slew
who would
    know)
      a sage
        gray or iron
gray, possibly
      a pale
    shade
of gainsboro,
    the un-
questionable color
      of gristle,
    or ships of
      the line
when I found him
  a day or
    two after
the fact
    in a faint,
      silver light
still comfortably
      seated up-
    right (his tower

too hallowed
  for some char
    to climb
up and discover)
  so I made my
ingress
      knock
    knock old
      sot through
  a niggling hole
    in the lower left
  sole of one
    thoughtfully
  shined, démodé
    brogue.

To the North Wind

At first darkness, an owl blesses the dead.
Within, cured game, the pale fire, and peace—

O come with morning the cold breath of sheets,
and slow love, huddled and mussed in my bed.

Notes

The opening epigraph is from Louis Simpson's "There Is."

"I Shall Name the Worms" on page 7 —
    The quotation is from [as freedom is a breakfastfood].

"Fat Worm" on page 46 —
    The quotation is Hamlet speaking to Claudius, Act IV, Scene III.

"Coy Worm" on page 52 —
    The quotation is from "To His Coy Mistress."

"Bedlam Songs" on pages 56–57 —
    Some of the language in these poems can be found in glossaries of Elizabethan slang.

"Mad Tom" on page 56 —
    Abraham Man: A beggar previously a patient of the Abraham ward at Bethlem Hospital

"Mad Maudlin" on page 57 —
    Chats: Gallows
    Chaveys: Children
    Tan: Abbreviation for Tanner, or sixpence
    Blue Bottles: Constables
    Gullies: The dupes of a grifter

Hailey Leithauser's debut collection, *Swoop*, won the Poetry Foundation's Emily Dickinson First Book Award and the Towson Prize for Literature. Her poems appear in *Agni*, the *Gettysburg Review, Poetry*, the *Yale Review,* and numerous other periodicals, and have been selected three times for *The Best American Poetry* anthology. She is a recipient of the Discovery/ the *Nation* Prize, the *River Styx* International Poetry Award, the Elizabeth Matchett Stover Award, and two Individual Artist Grants from the Maryland State Arts Council. She lives quite lazily at the edge of a precipitous wooded ravine a few miles north of Washington, DC, and teaches at the West Chester Poetry Conference.

ALSO FROM ABLE MUSE PRESS

Jacob M. Appel, *The Cynic in Extremis – Poems*

William Baer, *Times Square and Other Stories;*
  New Jersey Noir – A Novel;
  New Jersey Noir: Cape May – A Novel

Lee Harlin Bahan, *A Year of Mourning (Petrarch) – Translation*

Melissa Balmain, *Walking in on People (Able Muse Book Award for Poetry)*

Ben Berman, *Strange Borderlands – Poems;*
  Figuring in the Figure – Poems

Lorna Knowles Blake, *Green Hill (Able Muse Book Award for Poetry)*

Michael Cantor, *Life in the Second Circle – Poems*

Catherine Chandler, *Lines of Flight – Poems*

William Conelly, *Uncontested Grounds – Poems*

Maryann Corbett, *Credo for the Checkout Line in Winter – Poems;*
  Street View – Poems

John Philip Drury, *Sea Level Rising – Poems*

Rhina P. Espaillat, *And after All – Poems*

Anna M. Evans, *Under Dark Waters: Surviving the* Titanic *– Poems*

D. R. Goodman, *Greed: A Confession – Poems*

Margaret Ann Griffiths, *Grasshopper – The Poetry of M A Griffiths*

Katie Hartsock, *Bed of Impatiens – Poems*

Elise Hempel, *Second Rain – Poems*

Jan D. Hodge, *Taking Shape – carmina figurata;*
  The Bard & Scheherazade Keep Company – Poems

Ellen Kaufman, *House Music – Poems*

Emily Leithauser, *The Borrowed World (Able Muse Book Award for Poetry)*

Carol Light, *Heaven from Steam – Poems*

Kate Light, *Character Shoes – Poems*

April Lindner, *This Bed Our Bodies Shaped – Poems*

Martin McGovern, *Bad Fame – Poems*

Jeredith Merrin, *Cup – Poems*

Richard Moore, *Selected Poems;*
  The Rule That Liberates: An Expanded Edition – Selected Essays

www.ablemusepress.com